————CONTE

GW01451352

CHOICE

Mona Arshi • *Mouth* • Chatto & Windus

RECOMMENDATIONS

Simon Armitage • *New Cemetery* • Faber & Faber
Dean Browne • *After Party* • Picador
John Burnside • *The Empire of Forgetting* • Cape
Sasha Debevec-McKenney • *Joy is My Middle Name* • Fitzcarraldo

SPECIAL COMMENDATION

Edited by Rachel Long and Caroline Bird
Something New: Alternative Poems for Alternative Weddings • Picador

TRANSLATION CHOICE

Yordan Efftimov • *The Heart Is Not a Creator*
Translated by Jonathan Dunne • Broken Sleep Books

PAMPHLET CHOICE

Ilisha Thiru Purcell • *What She Said* • Verve Poetry Press

Poetry Book Society

CHOICE SELECTORS RECOMMENDATION SPECIAL COMMENDATION	YOMI ŞODE & VICTORIA KENNEFICK
TRANSLATION SELECTOR	SHIVANEE RAMLOCHAN
PAMPHLET SELECTORS	YOUSIF M. QASMIYEH & ALYCIA PIRMOHAMED
CONTRIBUTORS	SOPHIE O'NEILL MEGAN ROBSON LEDBURY CRITICS THE WRITING SQUAD ISOBEL DILLON
EDITORIAL & DESIGN	ALICE KATE MULLEN

Poetry Book Society Memberships

Choice

4 Books a Year: 4 Choice books & 4 *Bulletins* (UK £65, Europe £85, ROW £120)

World Poetry

8 Books: 4 Choices, 4 Translation books & 4 *Bulletins* (£98, £160, £190)

Complete

24 Books: 4 Choices, 16 Recommendations, 4 Translations & 4 *Bulletins* (£230, £290, £360)

Single copies of the *Bulletin* £12.99

Cover Artwork: Alexey Kondakov, *You Can't Even Imagine It*
Featuring original artworks from Frederic Leighton's *Electra at the Tomb of Agamemnon*
Instagram: @alksko Website: www.store.alksko.com

Supported using public funding by
ARTS COUNCIL ENGLAND

MIX
Paper | Supporting responsible forestry
FSC www.fsc.org FSC® C014866

Poetry Book Society | Milburn House | Dean Street | Newcastle upon Tyne | NE1 1LF
0191 230 8100 | enquiries@poetrybooksociety.co.uk

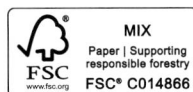

LETTER FROM THE PBS

I write with sadness. This is my last PBS letter before I move on from Inpress and the Poetry Book Society and hand the baton to the next wonderful leader, so please forgive a few words of reflection. The PBS has had its home in Newcastle for nine years now, and I feel a huge sense of pride in what the team have achieved in that time. We still exist! We attract new readers! We support amazing new poets, writers and reviewers! And we promote, not just new poets, but all poets from emerging voices to national treasures.

Inpress took on this amazing society because we could not imagine a world without these essential recommendations and endorsements. Our poet-selectors perform a Herculean task reading all the submissions and more importantly deciding on the selections – a job I would be incapable of doing, as I am generally in awe of anyone who can write poetry. The biggest thank you goes to you: our PBS members for your continued support. You are as essential to us as the poets themselves (more important, but don't tell the poets that). Without your commitment there would be no PBS; we salute you!

As ever, we have a fabulous selection this Autumn. Recommendations include a posthumous collection from John Burnside, the latest from our UK Poet Laureate and two absolutely stunning debuts. The Special Commendation is not just for those planning a wedding. I cannot wait to read this selection of modern and alternative love poems. And congratulations to our Pamphlet Choice, Ilisha Thiru Purcell who hails from our home of Newcastle. Mona Arshi's brilliant Autumn Choice *Mouth* was announced at the Jaipur Literature Festival in London at The British Library in June; a wonderful event which we would strongly recommend our readers attend in future, if you haven't already.

And while we're on events, as I write, we have just held our first online PBS Summer Showcase which was a huge success. A massive thank you to everyone who attended and our poets Fiona Benson, Isabelle Baafi, Victoria Kennefick and Pascale Petit for taking part. The Autumn Showcase will be at 7pm on the 8th October on Youtube featuring Simon Armitage, Mona Arshi and Sasha Debevec-McKenney. Keep an eye on our website for more details. Wishing you all the best for future *Bulletins* and mailouts, and may poetry continue to bring you great joy.

SOPHIE O'NEILL
PBS & INPRESS MANAGING DIRECTOR

MEET OUR SELECTORS

Victoria Kennefick: "What resonates with us in poetry changes as the seasons change, and alters as we move through our own cycles of death and rebirth, via the uncomfortably beautiful, and exposing, transitional in-between space of Autumn. This season is ripe with books about space and place, death and life, dark and light, all those in-betweens, that only poetry can truly illuminate. Be not afraid to step into the leaves of these magnificent books – they will bring you joy, they will tide you over."

Yomi Ṣode: "The Autumn Selections have been the perfect gateway in what's been a difficult period for me. These collections, ranging from joy to grief, offer poems to escape, think and, at times, breathe through. Very timely. I'm thankful."

TRANSLATION

Shivanee Ramlochan is a Trinidadian writer. Her debut collection *Everyone Knows I Am a Haunting* (Peepal Tree Press) was shortlisted for the Forward Prize. Her poems are anthologised in *100 Queer Poems* (Faber); *After Sylvia* (Nine Arches Press) and *Across Borders: New Poetry from the Commonwealth* (Verve Poetry Press).

PAMPHLETS

Yousif M. Qasmiyeh: "There was a timeless intimacy to these Autumn pamphlets: eternal gifts to my senses, exploring the mythical and the bodily, the exploratory and confessional, the unsettling secrets of living and departing. Together, they reaffirm how poetry is formed and reformed out of the clay of our old and newly emerging paths... As I read, I am reminded: what a privilege it is to breathe alongside other people's words".

Alycia Pirmohamed is the author of the PBS Recommendation *Another Way to Split Water,* Pamphlet Choice *Hinge* and a Nan Shepherd prize winning non-fiction book *A Beautiful and Vital Place.* She teaches at the University of Cambridge and co-founded the Scottish BPOC Writers Network.

MEET OUR REVIEWERS

NASIM REBECCA ASL is an award-winning Glasgow-based poet. Her debut pamphlet *Nemidoonam* was released by Verve Poetry Press in 2023. Nasim was shortlisted for the 2024 Forward Poetry Prize for Best Single Poem – Performed.

DAVE COATES is a critic and essayist based in Edinburgh. He was a co-organiser of the Ledbury Critics Programme and is published in *Poetry Review, Poetry London, The Stinging Fly, Extra Teeth, catflap, spamzine*. He has reviewed for the *Bulletin* since 2021.

JENNY DANES is a poet and facilitator whose work has appeared in *Poetry Wales, The Rialto, Magma, Under the Radar, Basket,* and *bath magg*. In 2016 she won The Poetry Business' New Poets Prize, and her pamphlet *Gaps* was published by Smith|Doorstop. Find out more at www.jennydanes.co.uk.

BETH DAVIES is the current Sheffield Poet Laureate. Her debut pamphlet *The Pretence of Understanding* was published by The Poetry Business in 2023 after winning the 2022 New Poets Prize. Find out more at bethdaviespoet.wordpress.com.

JASMINE GRAY is a Northern writer with art criticism and poetry published in *Anthropocene, The London Magazine*, and *The Double Negative*. She has published two pamphlets with Broken Sleep Books, *Let's Photograph Girls Enjoying Life* (2019) and *Open Your Mouth* (2023).

KAYLEIGH JAYSHREE is a poet and reviewer. She is an alumna of the Roundhouse Collective and performed poetry at Glastonbury Festival. She has published reviews in *PN Review* and *Ink Sweat & Tears*. Her pamphlet is due out with fourteen poems.

GREGORY KEARNS is based in Liverpool. He was published in *Bath Magg, The Mersey Review* and *Not About Now* and has worked with English Heritage, No Dice Collective and Tmesis Theatre. He hosts The Poems We Made Along The Way podcast.

ROSE SCHIERIG is a poet and MA Writing Poetry student at Newcastle University. She graduated with a BA in English Literature with Creative Writing from Newcastle University in 2024. You can read her writing @fromrosamund on Instagram. She recently joined The Writing Squad.

SHASH TREVETT is a poet and translator of Tamil poetry into English. Her collection *The Naming of Names* was published by Smith|Doorstop (2024). She is a Ledbury Critic and a Trustee of *Modern Poetry in Translation*.

MONA ARSHI

Mona Arshi's debut poetry collection *Small Hands* won the Forward Prize for Best First Collection in 2015. Her second collection *Dear Big Gods* was published in 2019 and her novel *Somebody Loves You* in 2021; the latter was shortlisted for The Goldsmiths Prize. She was appointed as Honorary Professor at the University of Liverpool and Fellow in Creative Arts at Trinity College, Cambridge, and is also co-editor of an anthology of nature poetry *Nature Matters* (Faber). Prior to her career in poetry, she worked as a human rights lawyer, often representing refugees and women fleeing domestic violence.

MOUTH

CHATTO & WINDUS | £12.99 | PBS PRICE £9.75

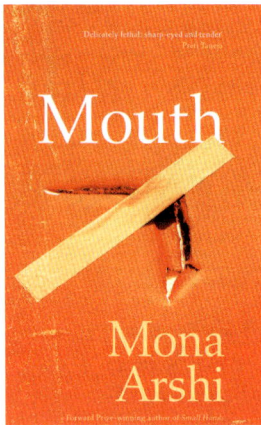

Mona Arshi's third collection solidifies her reputation as a poet who masterfully delves into trauma, identity, and the complexities of human experience to amplify the narratives of those often suppressed, suffering and sidelined. This is a compelling exploration of voice, silence and survival.

> Say it, he says
> raising his axe.
> I bite my tongue so
> it bleeds first.

The opening poems brilliantly interrogate the origins of violence, as Arshi uses her poetic magnifying glass to expose the small cruelties and impulsivities we commit daily with tender precision. In 'Yellows' the speaker, overwhelmed by the bright "blizzard of yellow" caused by rapeseed pollen on a train, impetuously, but knowingly, tips a resting bee, and her attendant soul, out of the window. With the passage of time, which Arshi deftly achieves, the speaker becomes more circumspect, more aligned with her intense sensitivity, the poet's sensibility perhaps, and this power is more positively and powerfully channelled elsewhere: into a karmic ritual that promotes healing or maybe, even, into a poem.

> I rescue petals from tea-cups,
> appease wasps at my table, praying
> they've all repaired themselves fully in
> the ancient ways...

The interconnectedness of all things is palpable throughout with startling and chilling examples of cause and effect. In 'Salt' the transgression seems minor, but is anything but: "Once as children, we did something terrible (too awful) to the snails." This superb poem contains the truth of children's innocent aggression and their burgeoning awareness that their actions inflict hurt, "tongues oiled with shame / when one of us asked whether those creatures felt pain". There is an undeniable mythical quality to these poems which speaks across the collection. The sequence 'Palace' reimagines the voices of women from the periphery of Greek tragedy, placing them centre stage to narrate stories of survival and loss: "look at our collapsed stories, shadows at your feet like shawled mothers." Silence becomes a profound form of expression, and Arshi suggests that "sometimes / language picks us clean." It is a breathtaking achievement to fearlessly and powerfully explore how words both reveal and conceal truths, through the container of poems, and make the white space sing.

| SELECTOR'S COMMENT

VICTORIA KENNEFICK

MONA ARSHI

Who uses language and who is unlanguaged is one of the defining questions of our time, particularly during war and its aftermath. And correspondingly there's a deeper interest in Classical texts. Anne Carson has spoken of this pull that drives us back to the Greeks as something like a "collective guilt" that we share through these poems and plays. Although novelists and playwrights have much to say, I've realised that the poet's task, on re-encountering these works, is an altogether different one. These texts put the poet in direct confrontation, in linguistic terms, with the dark face of our times. The silent women I'm concerned with recovering in *Mouth* are Eurydice: the bereaved mother and wife in Sophocles' *Antigone*; and the enslaved girl Chryseis, Agamemnon's "war bride" from the Trojan myths, who violently present us with a side of war that is both present and palpable.

Sophocles' pressure-cooker of a play is a gift for a poet, because apart from the moral and philosophical ideas in the play, it is also a simple story of a girl who is grieving and so utterly devoid of a path for mourning. What happens when poets alloy the dark themes of ancient stories with the exigencies of our despairing times? It was like a "pneumatic drill trying to bite and shudder. Call it a rage for order", discovered Seamus Heaney, as he composed his poetic sequence 'Mycenae Lookout' which ferried centuries of devastation in rhymed triplets. It's a work where the world of Agamemnon's return home mixes with contemporary Northern Irish conflicts. The works of Homer and Sophocles gift us an imaginative legacy which, as it were, leaves the live cables lying on the war-torn ground; or, to put in another way, the ancient tent pegs must stay in place whilst the poets chisel away at the hard earth.

Restoring voice to the silent isn't easy. I see it as an ethical task, working alongside these mythic women to recover what's hidden in ancient storage. We must be careful, sensitive, as we walk in the ruins of the unlanguaged: it's akin to palpating a vein before drawing blood and we must forgive these women their silences.

MONA RECOMMENDS

Sandeep Parmar, *Eidolon* (Shearsman Books); Seamus Heaney, *The Spirit Level* (Faber); Derek Walcott, *Omeros* (Faber); Rabindranath Tagore, *Chitra* (Macmillan); Alice Oswald, *Memorial* (Faber); Anne Carson, *Antigonick* (New Directions); Ilya Kaminsky, *Deaf Republic* (Faber); Wisława Szymborska, *View with a Grain of Sand* (Faber); Valzhyna Mort, *Music for the Dead and Resurrected* (Bloomsbury Press).

ANTIGONE'S PRIZE

The children are collecting shells again:
their thin ankles planted in the sand
against the tide's swell.

They bring me their milky broken offerings
and other glazed perfections
which have the primal quality of newborns,

a silvery rainbowed mouth threatens to
pour out its secrets.
Another tongueless gift shows tracks on

its back where currents lusted while the fish
stared and stared.
But this one is my daughter's favourite:

she's already begun to adopt its perforated
useless rooms.
No one else wants this shell, but my darling

girl is holding it tight in her small fist.
She has a desire to nurture it. She slips it
in her pocket; strumming it with her thumb.

TO A MAN WITH A HAMMER EVERYTHING LOOKS LIKE A NAIL

In war the mothers have all the language.
My greatest fear is that I will wake up
tomorrow and not fear anything again.
I won't have to poke awake my uncrying
children who will be up at dawn scavenging
on mounds before even the crows land.
What is it like to be without light?
In the bomb shelter we trace our circadian rhythms.
Oh dearest breath don't leave me now. I play
Ludo with my son and my lungs are on fire
and the bombing hasn't even started.
Am I winning? He asks eagerly in the torchlight.
I catch a glint of a white tooth. It's an age-old language;
Yes I tell him *yes. You are winning.*

SIMON ARMITAGE

Simon Armitage was born in West Yorkshire and is Professor of Poetry at the University of Leeds. His collections, which have received numerous prizes and awards, include *Seeing Stars* (2010), *Blossomise* (2024) and his acclaimed translation of *Sir Gawain and the Green Knight* (2007). He writes extensively for television and radio, and is the author of two novels and the non-fiction bestsellers *All Points North* (1998), *Walking Home* (2012) and *Walking Away* (2015). His theatre works include *The Last Days of Troy*, performed at Shakespeare's Globe in 2014. From 2015-19, he served as Professor of Poetry at the University of Oxford, and he was awarded the Queen's Gold Medal for Poetry in 2018. Simon Armitage is the UK Poet Laureate.

RECOMMENDATION

NEW CEMETERY

FABER & FABER | £14.99 | PBS PRICE £11.25

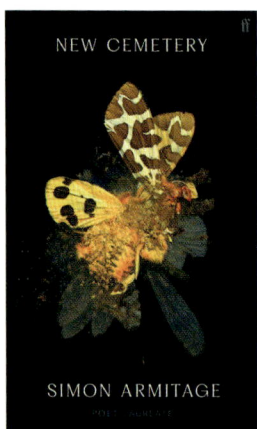

"I hadn't intended to write poems about the cemetery – let alone so many – but once four or five pieces had taken shape, they seemed to suggest a way forward." Simon Armitage opens *New Cemetery* with a note that feels like a quiet confession. The collection is born from the local authority's proposed conversion of cow fields into a cemetery – an act that unsettled the surrounding community. Armitage constructs a poetic journey, one that invites the reader to sit beside him, observing this changing landscape. As readers, we find ourselves peering through windows, we are the neighbour, or, at times, a mirror. We are measuring how far the site has come, or sitting quietly on a bench, watching strangers mourn loved ones, on ground that once felt familiar. We become a kind of confessional, silent, reflective, through which Armitage processes his thoughts and grief. Curiosity lingers throughout, gently compelling us to look closer:

> Site inspection
> and weather report: light snow
> fringing cemetery lanes,
>
> old ice
> lending all graves
> a pewter-cum-frosted glass-
>
> cum-marquisette frame.
> For 'altocumulus'
> read 'sparrowhawk strike'.
>
> Two new headstones:
> one guitar-shaped
> with adjustable knobs
>
> for VOLUME and TONE,
> the other carved
> as a football shirt.

Grief underpins everything, from the pandemic to the poet's surroundings, and the personal loss of his father. Armitage's response is less abstract than in earlier works, as he notes in 'Moth', marked by urgency and honesty. It's this drive to confront what's personal, that makes the collection resonate strongly. A feeling that I find deeply relatable.

YOMI ȘODE

| SELECTOR'S COMMENT

SIMON ARMITAGE

The poems in this collection accumulated very slowly over several years. Across that period I'd been working on a number of large-scale projects for theatre, radio, and television, as well as taking on many commissions and residencies, and two very demanding translations – *The Owl and The Nightingale* and *Gilgamesh*. When it came to individual poems it probably suited me to write shorter and more portable pieces, things I could partially compose in my mind while travelling and having to constantly switch focus. Like all short poems, though, they turned out to be more demanding than longer ones – more conspicuous, more attention seeking, more needy. And I certainly hadn't intended writing so many – maybe a hundred or so in the end, before I sat down with my editor, Lavinia Singer, and found the book within the book.

The starting point was my Local Authority declaring its intentions to turn a patch of pretty cow fields at the top of a hill into a cemetery. My neighbours were horrified and protested, but I found myself more inclined towards a graveyard than an industrial estate or fifty or so new houses – I'm a poet, I like it quiet, the dead don't talk back. Actually they do, and more than a few of the poems are broken conversations with the departed, including my dad, who died four years ago.

During various phases of lockdown, when outdoor recreation was restricted to the immediate locality, the path through the emerging cemetery became the only option, so to some extent the book forms a journal, and a barometer of world events, not least the Covid-19 pandemic and it's effect on burials and funeral rituals. Moths feature strongly, and, as you would expect from a collection with this title and subject matter, it's hilarious.

SIMON RECOMMENDS

Richard Scott, *That Broke into Shining Crystals* (Faber & Faber); Fawzia Muradali Kane, *Guaracara* (Carcanet); Caroline Bird, *Ambush at Still Lake* (Carcanet); Martin Malone, *The Unreturning* (Shoestring Press); Geoff Hattersley, *Harmonica* (Wrecking Ball Press); Gillian Clarke, *The Silence* (Carcanet); Brian Eno and Bette A., *what art does: an unfinished theory* (Faber & Faber); Sam Lee, *songdreaming* L.P. (Cooking Vinyl Limited); Major Jackson, *Razzle Dazzle: New and Selected Poems 2002-2022* (W.W. Norton).

RECOMMENDATION

[CLOUDED BUFF]

The new cemetery's shaping up.
    A stone-built lychgate
        doubles as bin store and toilet block.

The departed are yet to arrive
    so the numbered plots lie undisturbed,
        but the roads are laid out:

avenues of virgin tarmac
    leading to turning circles and cul-de-sacs.
        And there's no barrier,

so day and night the site crawls
    with dog walkers, adulterers
        and learner drivers.

[BEADED CHESTNUT]

We blundered
    onto a country lane
        by a NO TRESPASSING sign,

bare legs buttoned
    with nettle stings
        and raked by thorns,

the green shield-bug
    a prefect badge
        on your white blouse,

the moon
    an ironic smile
        in the afternoon sky.

Somewhere behind us:
    a flattened nest
        in a cereal crop

where a pair of otters
    had topped and tailed.
        Had not.

The summer of couldn't-care-less,
    didn't know our oats
        from our barley,

barley from wheat,
    wheat from corn.
        Didn't know we were born.

DEAN BROWNE

Dean Browne is from Tipperary, Ireland, and lives in Cork. He received the Geoffrey Dearmer Prize in 2021. His pamphlet *Kitchens at Night* won the Poetry Business International Pamphlet Competition and was published by Smith|Doorstop in 2022. His poems have appeared in *The London Magazine, New York Review of Books, Poetry Magazine, Poetry Review, The Stinging Fly,* and elsewhere. *After Party* is his debut collection.

AFTER PARTY

PICADOR | £12.99 | PBS PRICE £9.75

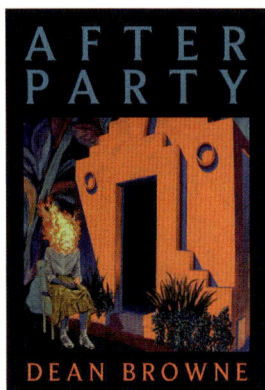

In a debut collection replete with stand-out poems like, 'Aide-Mémoire', 'Flinch,' 'Butternut Squash' and 'Oink,' Dean Browne's *After Party* also includes two elegiac poems: 'The Infinite', in memory of Charles Simic, and 'Pinball,' honouring the surrealist genius of the late great Donegal-born poet, Matthew Sweeney:

> …he didn't want a headstone –
> no wings, no spidery gothic script –
> instead, an old pinball machine
> should mark the place of his grave.

It is a fitting and moving tribute that speaks to Sweeney's fable-like and humorous sensibilities and points to Browne as his natural successor in the realm of what Sweeney called in an interview with Lidia Vianu, "alternative realism." Browne, however, has a new and arresting perspective and voice that are distinctly his own. In his imagistic narratives a leg sets off on a long train journey in 'The Leg'; a Parisian alley cat is launched into space in 'To Félicette' and earthbound lovers attempt to connect while their inner lives prove unbridgeable. *After Party* exists in the space between domesticity and imagination, the dreamt and the actual – those semi-hallucinatory liminal places we all fall into from time to time. In 'Aide-Mémoire' a goat appears with a message, a chilli prompts metaphysical questions in 'Approach to Chilli' and in 'Pine Box in the Flea Market' the box in question contains Plathian multitudes and a chilling nod to mortality:

> Inside? Maybe a bunch of shrunken heads;
> a rosary of goats' teeth, bone blushing;
> a pair of rusty, rubber-handled pliers;
> the peekaboo of a tarantula –
> you are a horsefly learning immensity
> at the brink of a donkey's ear.

Browne's poetic lens can adjust its focus to capture the smallest flea, while also panning out to take in a whole scene, as in 'Afternaut', "cracking cloves from the provocative / bouquet on a chopping-board in Cork, / watched from the window by one star." In this realm of half-light and in-betweenness Browne can see everything and dissect it with wry humour and heartbreaking clarity, like the true host of an after party where perception and reality blur at the edges, all is wonderfully strange and yet makes perfect sense.

VICTORIA KENNEFICK

DEAN BROWNE

I think of poetry as an encounter, not so much transcription of experience as transformation. Like a dream, poetry can be a speed date with the unconscious, that proto-imagiste. The main thing is that I aspire to surprise myself in the act of writing. By that I mean I write myself into a strange place, that ideally relocates me, and hopefully the reader, in a new relationship to ordinary life for a moment. Like an otter with their second eyelid, the "nictitating membrane", that closes over and protects their eyes when they go underwater, enabling them to go deeper, one is trying to get down to that deeper, oozy place where the unrationalisable magic is. The epigraph for *After Party* is from 'Spring and All' by William Carlos Williams: "To whom then am I addressed? To the imagination".

Across the poems of the collection, I often wanted to begin somewhere unlikely, even inauspicious, and trust in the arrival of mystery resources to carry the poem, while keeping true to its own weird inner logic; I never want to know where it's going in advance. "A poem is about something the way a cat is about a house", said Allen Grossman. The drama of this process is played out in the opening poem, 'Aide-Memoire': "That's not very original I think but I'll see where it leads". I was interested in finding form for the drift of association we all experience, in all its exuberance and arbitrariness and feeling.

Lorca's *Poet in New York* had a profound impact on me when I was twenty one or so. I thought, this is possible? Akin to that work, *After Party* is an elegiac collection – elegising a poet friend and teacher, for example in 'Pinball', but also school friends lost to suicide or substances, in 'Rachael's Coat Inside Out'. I hope the title of the collection has resonance in that respect, while being alive to poetry as the "electric, /... magic field" Bill Knott wrote of, "like the space / between a sleepwalker's outheld arms" – the poem is a space for inquisitiveness and humour. I consider it an honour and a huge affirmation that the Poetry Book Society has chosen *After Party* as a recommendation, and I am grateful.

DEAN RECOMMENDS

Scott McKendry, *Gub* (Corsair); Caroline Bird, *Ambush at Still Lake* (Carcanet); Thomas McCarthy, *Plenitude* (Carcanet); Joey Connolly, *The Recycling* (Carcanet); Susannah Dickey, *Isdal* (Picador); Zaffar Kunial, *England's Green* (Faber); Michael Dooley, *In Spring We Turned to Water* (Doire); Gustav Parker Hibbitt, *High Jump as Icarus Story* (Banshee Press); Maurice Riordan, *Selected Poems* (Faber); John Mee, *The Blue in the Blue Marble* (Templar); Karen Solie, *Wellwater* (Picador); Patrick Cotter, *Quality Control at the Miracle Factory* (Dedalus); Russell Edson, *Little Mr Prose Poem: Selected Poems* (Boa Editions); Denise Riley, *Say Something Back* (Picador); James Tate, *Hell, I Love Everybody: 82 Poems* (Carcanet); Paul Farley, *When It Rained For A Million Years* (Picador); Bill Knott, *The Naomi Poems: Corpse and Beans* (Black Ocean).

As children we played with the edge of fire

FLIES

The flies kept manifesting *ex nihilo*.
Thought I was equipped with a good swatter
that would last forever. I was wrong.
This was inconvenient but not fatal.
The flipflop I weaponized was effective
and music, the slain corpses falling
like arpeggios on a glockenspiel
and that was a result. Loud about my ears,
settling in my hair, down which each of
my secret thoughts ran, I felt them frolic
and wanted to die. Why were flies
so officious in this town? Enough landed
upon my friend once to carry him off
over the roofs, like in a Chagall –
but I clapped them dead, and the ones
I couldn't kill I turned into metaphor

JOHN BURNSIDE

John Burnside was among the most acclaimed writers of his generation. His novels, short stories, poetry and memoirs won numerous awards, including the Geoffrey Faber Memorial, Saltire Scottish Book of the Year and, in 2023, he received the David Cohen Prize for a lifetime's achievement in literature. In 2011 *Black Cat Bone* won both the Forward and the T.S. Eliot Prizes for poetry.

RECOMMENDATION

THE EMPIRE OF FORGETTING

CAPE | £13.00 | PBS PRICE £9.75

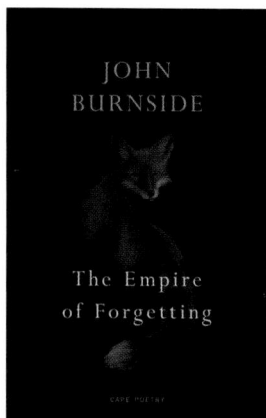

Having recently received the news of my grandmother's passing, the timing of reading *The Empire of Forgetting*, the posthumous new collection by John Burnside, felt coincidental. I had done everything but take time to mourn, to sit still and reflect on her life.

Immersing myself in Burnside's words, I found myself drawn, not only into his poetic world, but also into memories of her. Though she wasn't a writer, I wished for something similar from her – a record of thought, a trace of inner life.

The Empire of Forgetting moves through time, nature, and the self, with mortality as a quiet but constant presence. Burnside's language is elegant and unflinching. There's a wisdom in his tone, as though he has walked through every season of life and returned with myth and clarity in hand.

> When all the books are gone, there will be
> nothing to remember but a single
> porch light at the far end of the road,
> where something live is moving in the snow,
> a woman, or a fox, it's hard to say.
>
> Last day of birdsong; salt rain in the trees;
> the echo of someone going about
> their business, making good or making hay
> – you never know for sure, although you know
> that something here is coming to an end:

It is never easy to face loss. Burnside's collection does not offer answers, but it gives voice to the liminal space between presence and absence. In the foreword, his long-standing editor and poetry publisher, Robin Robertson writes, "It was one of the privileges of my life to work with John Burnside."

For readers and fans of his work, I'm sure it is bittersweet to read this new offering. The thirtieth book in his remarkable career, *The Empire of Forgetting* is a fitting, moving legacy.

YOMI ȘODE

A TRIBUTE TO JOHN BURNSIDE

In the thirty four years I knew, and worked with, John, I was astonished by his fluid imagination, his range and curiosity, his creative gifts. That huge, generous heart. His endless contradictions. He resented the imposed empiricism of being offered only five senses, when he felt there were more. He held imagination as his one most crucial tool – or weapon – in the fight for art, for settlement, beauty and grace – in the search for a fleeting glimpse of that ephemeral vision, the glamourie. This Scottish word, "glamourie" – Anglicised to "glamour" – means a fleeting enchantment, or magic, and I think John was always drawn to that concept of a conjured charm or presence that came from the spirit-world, and he was watching for it constantly. That liminal light.

His work was both intimately personal yet universal and profound – often moving through stages of vulnerability, turbulence, terror and desire, to artistic positions that were sensitive and highly alert. He risked everything for his art and its integrity – always arriving at a new and original understanding of beauty, of truth, or offering a better angle to view the world – through the even older eyes of nature, myth and magic. Every poem for him was a transformation. Metamorphosis. Transfiguration.

I was amazed when I found out how he wrote poems: in his head, out walking – "on the lips" as Mandelstam called it – and let them stay in his head, marinating, until they were ready to appear. He said he could carry a long section of a poem there, for days – while it was still warm and malleable. When he finally transcribed the poem to paper it had already settled into a kind of music. As a result, his work never felt forced, or fussed over, just mysterious and natural as breathing.

In his last years, after his sleep problems, his catastrophic heart failure in 2020, his recovery, and then the award of the David Cohen Prize for a lifetime achievement (...) – my sense is that John felt he had done what he'd set out to do. There was completion. For someone who wanted to disappear as a child – to be *Living Nowhere* (the title of one of his novels)... I believe John reached a place of acceptance, completion and peace.

(...) I'll finish with these lines from John's third memoir, *I Put a Spell on You*: "It might sound sentimental to say it, but we are blessed by the dead, and we know that we are, in spite of our protestations to the contrary. They leave spaces in our lives that, for some of us, are the closest thing to sacred we ever know. They are there and then they are gone and, after a time, we come to see a certain elegance in that – the elegance of a magic trick, say, where the conjurer rehearses the vanishing act that we must all accomplish sooner or later."

ROBIN ROBERTSON, JOHN BURNSIDE'S EDITOR

NATURE STUDY

It might have been a puzzle, or a form
of absence we had yet to comprehend:

nature table, blueprints for a way of being
animal, a brightness still to come

implicit in a clutch of plover's eggs,
a bowl of leaves, a weft of bone and feathers;

and yet we were less present in our world
than snail shells, or a slip

of minnow at the bottom of a jar,
forgotten, iridescent, almost gone,

but dreaming, till the end,
of light and rain.

THE EMPIRE OF FORGETTING

I

Out in the field where, once,
we played Dead Man's Fall,

the others are being called
through the evening dusk

– Kenny and Marek, the Corrigans, Alex McClure –
mothers and sisters calling them home for tea

from kitchens warmed with steam and buttered toast,
broth on the hot plate, ham hough and yellow lentils.

Barely a wave, then they're gone, till no one is left,
and the dark from the woods closes in on myself alone,

the animals watching, the older gods
couched in the shadows.

Decades ago, I suppose,
though I cannot be sure.

I have waited here, under the stars,
for the longest time.

SASHA DEBEVEC-McKENNEY

Sasha Debevec-McKenney's poems have appeared in *The New Yorker*, *The New York Review of Books* and *The Yale Review*. She was the 2020-21 Jay C. and Ruth Halls Poetry Fellow at the University of Wisconsin and is currently a creative writing fellow at Emory University.

JOY IS MY MIDDLE NAME

FITZCARRALDO | £12.99 | PBS PRICE £9.75

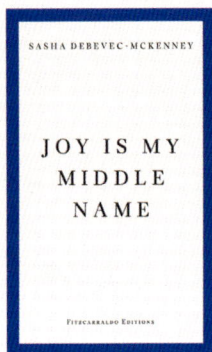

Sasha Debevec-Mckenney's *Joy Is My Middle Name* is a magnificent, radical debut from a bold and exciting new voice. Its sparky originality is established by titles that are poems in themselves, 'YOUR BRAIN IS NOT A PRISON!', 'SAMPLE OF MYSELF,' 'WHAT AM I AFRAID OF?', '*ALONE*DERLAND' which not only hint at a fresh perspective in writing the self but also point to a certain tenderness that feels like an act of rebellion in an age like this.

The contents page is bookended by the most wonderful and unexpected acknowledgments poem, 'DEBTS, SOURCES, NOTES' after Robert Caro, the American journalist and biographer of United States political figures like former President Lyndon Johnson, who appears unforgettably in 'WHEN I MET SHARON OLDS SHE TOLD ME TO WRITE A POEM ABOUT LBJ'S PENIS' and elsewhere:

> LBJ is in hell with all the other presidents!
> On a burning hilltop, in a graveyard
> full of flaccid legacies, they wave
> their penises like white flags.

This remarkable piece is so intimate and executed with such a conversational ease that pervades the entire collection – at turns hilarious, heartbreaking, subversive, courageous and eye-opening. Debevec-McKenney has the uncanny ability to make the reader feel like they are experiencing first-hand the brilliantly chaotic and profoundly intelligent process of a writer at work, such is the generosity of spirit, unmatched ambition and exceptional skill of a poet who explores femininity, sex, race, addiction, capitalism and pop culture through a buzzy, boisterous, brilliant lens that wants you to see and celebrate that, despite it all, in spite of ourselves, "Tangerine is finally in! Joy is in! Let it in!"

The quotidian and the historic, the personal and the political, interior and external experience, co-exist awkwardly and perfectly in this inspiring patchwork. The opening poem, a prelude to the book, is a humorous and breathless cento, 'CENTO FOR THE NIGHT I TRIED STAND-UP'. One must agree with Terrance Hayes when he says, "*Joy Is My Middle Name* is bold as hell. It's revitalizing."

VICTORIA KENNEFICK

SASHA DEBEVEC-McKENNEY

I remember the first time I read a poem by Lucille Clifton 'in the inner city' – I was maybe fifteen years old. The poem is short, repetitive and a deceptively simple description of a place. And I understood it! Poems were allowed to make sense! I honestly did not know that before I read that poem. Lucille quickly became my favorite poet. I read from her *Collected Poems* every morning, thirteen years later, living in Brooklyn and doing my MFA in poetry at NYU. I wrote some of *Joy is My Middle Name* there, extremely overstimulated and twenty eight years old.

Then I moved back to Wisconsin and lived on a lake which I could hear from my bedroom. Now I'm thirty five. The book is like a museum of my life so far, a fictional retelling of my mistakes, heartbreaks, obsessions, all the fun I had and everything that upset me. I say "anger brings me to the page" as a joke sometimes, but it really does. I think of myself as part of the Confessional tradition, although poetry is legally fiction and I am a huge liar for the sake of emotional truth. I think this book fits in with addiction memoirs that don't end with the writer being clean, sober and completely fixed.

I've been obsessed with American history and politics since I was a little girl, I've struggled with my body image since I was a little girl: I'll write about that forever. These poems were written as a way for me to process my feelings and maybe to teach the reader a little something about American history. They were written to impress the boys I like and to make my friends laugh. I hope they make you laugh too.

SASHA RECOMMENDS

Rachael Allen, *God Complex* (Faber & Faber); Hera Lindsay Bird, *Hera Lindsay Bird* (Penguin); Diane Seuss, *Modern Poetry* (Fitzcarraldo); Adania Shibli, *Minor Detail* (Fitzcarraldo Editions); Heather Christle, *Paper Crowns* (Hachette); Victoria Kennefick, *Eat or We Both Starve* (Carcanet Press); Holly Pester, *Comic Timing* (Granta); Nick Laird, *Up Late* (Faber & Faber).

RECOMMENDATION

I THOUGHT MY LIFE WAS OVER

I thought my life was over but it was only a pandemic.
I fled the city, I couldn't even sleep there one more night.
It was March 13th. I fell asleep in my suburb,
Breonna Taylor fell asleep in her city. Now
that she's dead, I know these details about her life.
She was going to turn 26 on June 5th, I was going to turn 30.
I didn't want to. I wasn't eating, but I had to shop.
I only went downstairs to wipe off my packages.
I overheard my father on a phone call with his doctor
who was saying, "Yes, for now, you're still prediabetic." For now.
For a week I thought about his belly crushing his lungs.
Somehow, his sixty-eighth birthday passed. I didn't kill him,
but we didn't hug. I kept preparing myself to lose.
I prepared myself to see so many dead black people.
Historically, I had to be prepared. I collected unemployment
while I complained. I was practically chanting it.
My life is over. Hers was. All those years
we celebrated together and didn't know it.
In my dreams, I wished for a birthday party.
I was wearing a pink feathered robe, I was the center of attention,
I was the piece of shit—why did I get to live?
I thought my life was over but it kept going.

HARTFORD HOSPITAL, NOVEMBER, BARACK OBAMA IS PRESIDENT

My grandmother rarely
called us by our real names
but you knew when she meant you.
I was the youngest girl
so I had the most names. Yes
her sentences had always
trailed off into little mysteries to me
but when she was dying

and the doctor asked her
what month it was
she said November
and I thought oh, good,
so she isn't dying
she knows it's November.
But she didn't know the year.
And she didn't know the President.
The doctor left. It was just me,
my brother and my grandmother

and the CNN anchor saying
JFK was killed fifty years ago
this month,
my grandmother saying
do they know who shot him yet,
my brother saying no,
and death pulling its drawstring,
closing us all inside.

Image: Eliza Squire-Bird

Image: Amaal Said

CAROLINE BIRD

RACHEL LONG

Caroline Bird is a poet and playwright. Her previous collections include *Rookie* (Carcanet, 2022) and *The Air Year* (2020). She won the Forward Prize for Best Collection in 2020, and has been shortlisted for the T.S. Eliot Prize, the Costa Book Awards, the Ted Hughes Award, the Polari Prize and the Dylan Thomas Prize. She won a Cholmondeley Award in 2023. Her seventh collection *Ambush at Still Lake* was published in 2024.

Rachel Long's debut collection *My Darling from the Lions* (Picador, 2020) was shortlisted for the Forward Prize for Best First Collection, the Costa Book Awards and The *Sunday Times* Young Writer of the Year Award.

SOMETHING NEW

PICADOR | £16.99 | PBS PRICE £12.75

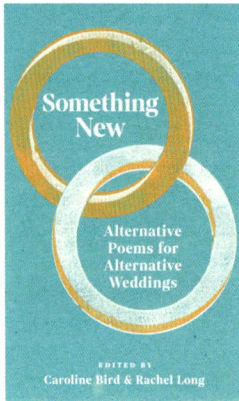

In *Something New: Alternative Poems for Alternative Weddings*, edited by Caroline Bird and Rachel Long, readers are invited into a world where wedding poems defy tradition. This collection is wild, tender, messy, and urgent – offering a refreshing alternative to the neat and conventional verses often shared at ceremonies. These are poems of autonomy, intimacy, and the emotional chaos of love, as it truly is, not how it's often staged. As in Kim Addonizio's 'Like That' – a poem filled with ominous imagery and fierce vulnerability.

> Love me like a wrong turn on a bad road late at night with
> no moon and no town anywhere

Or Emily Berry's 'It was as if I were asleep' where love pulses with the blood's grief and strength:

> ...but as long as
> I live, come to me, as long as my love has the
> strength of the blood that gives life

These aren't just poems; they're raw, alive, and unapologetically honest.

Scrolling through videos one evening, I came across a couple so present in their love that for a moment it felt like time paused. In a world often too heavy or too fast, these moments – and these poems – offer a space to breathe. Reminding us that weddings are more than rituals. They're about connection, authenticity and creating new traditions.

Yes, the joy of jumping the broom, spraying dollars, or the candy dance, still resonates, but this anthology proposes something additional: a poetry of now. One which aunties, uncles, friends, and chosen family – all swept into the celebration – can share. With over one hundred poems, *Something New* is more than a book. It's a gateway, a pause, a place to escape into when life becomes too serious. And in that space, perhaps, we find not only love, but also ourselves – seen, heard, and held.

YOMI ȘODE

TWENTY-ONE LOVE POEMS BY ADRIENNE RICH

II

I wake up in your bed. I know I have been dreaming.
Much earlier, the alarm broke us from each other,
you've been at your desk for hours. I know what I dreamed:
our friend the poet comes into my room
where I've been writing for days,
drafts, carbons, poems are scattered everywhere,
and I want to show her one poem
which is the poem of my life. But I hesitate,
and wake. You've kissed my hair
to wake me. *I dreamed you were a poem,*
I say, *a poem I wanted to show someone...*
and I laugh and fall dreaming again
of the desire to show you to everyone I love,
to move openly together
in the pull of gravity, which is not simple,
which carries the feathered grass a long way down the
    upbreathing air.

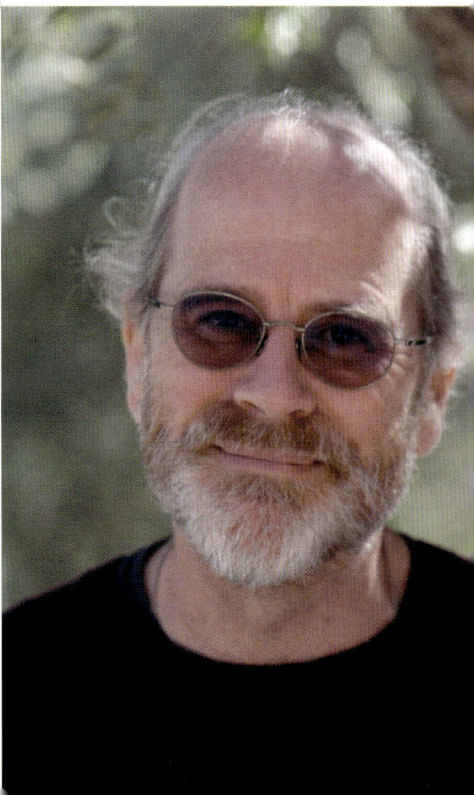

YORDAN EFFTIMOV

JONATHAN DUNNE

Yordan Efftimov (born 1971 in Razgrad, Bulgaria) is a poet, literary historian, and assistant professor in Theory of Literature at New Bulgarian University, Sofia. He has written eight poetry books. *The Heart Is Not a Creator* won the Ivan Nikolov National Award for Poetry Book of the Year (2013) and the Hristo Fotev National Award for Poetry (2014). He is also the author of popular science books, including *Quarantinscapes and Other Micro-Essays* (2021).

Jonathan Dunne is a graduate in Classics from the University of Oxford. He has translated more than eighty books from Bulgarian, Catalan, Galician and Spanish. He directs Small Stations Press, the main publisher of Galician literature in English. He has written on the theology of language, most recently *Seven Brief Lessons on Language* (2023). You can find out more on his website www.stonesofithaca.com.

THE HEART IS NOT A CREATOR

YORDAN EFFTIMOV, TRANSLATED BY JONATHAN DUNNE

BROKEN SLEEP BOOKS | £14.99 | PBS PRICE £11.25

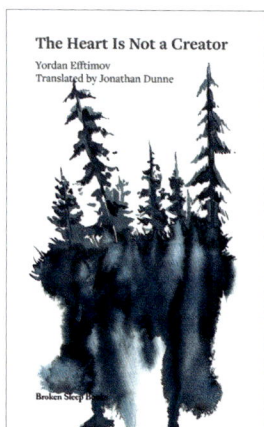

Layered in the scenes of these poems are everyday, human crimes: a body gone missing, a love wrung out to dry without satisfaction. Yordan Efftimov's *The Heart is Not a Creator* presents them to us without moralising, or conjecture as to our human ends. Our fates, the poems say plainly, are rooted in death, rushing up to meet us. What grounds the book in a sincere and irrefutable pleasure is how it meets that premise with a toothed curiosity.

Translated from the Bulgarian by Jonathan Dunne, Efftimov's speakers are observers and storytellers, garrulous and laconic by turns. Each invites us less to know them, as they do to implicate the reader in a world they are, themselves, discovering. Some of these journeys are glacial, historic: 'House on the Waves' pitches us towards the tragedy of a young child's death, occasioned by walking on frozen-over sea. The youth remains unknowable in death, even when he has morphed past immediate mourning into haunting legend.

> The bones of the anonymous child
> gave off absolutely no fragrance.

Yet Efftimov's diction, upheld by Dunne's crisp, taut translation, fends off a cursory balefulness in favour of a questioning acuity, even in the documentation of dire – sometimes heartbreaking – times. So many of these poems are expansively oceanic, perched on seaside resorts, tumbling into leviathan-filled chasms, conjuring:

> Huge waves like full lips. Waves like ocean waterfalls. Waves that
> invade like a shower of kisses and don't let you breathe.

Titular insistence signals out several poems, each called 'The Heart is Not a Creator'. Call this existential, or metaphysical, depending on your inclination: the collection's wondering thesis is that the heart cannot generate newness, nor, the poems persuade us, rooted in nothing less than total attention to the world, can the heart destroy what we engineer.

SHIVANEE RAMLOCHAN

IT'S INSULTING WHEN YOU DO NOT LOVE

You stare blurry-eyed
at all those rushing into the water.
Splashing
with sought-after joy,
barely stepping forward,
relaxed, as if they believe, drifting,
fathers performing world
acrobatic tricks for their sons,
with their backs to us.

Horizon gazers –
huge anchorless
caves.

You hear their hearts –
each has their own truth.
And truth is just the appearance of desire.
No more,
no less.
World.

PAMPHLET CHOICE

Ilisha Thiru Purcell is an award-winning Sri Lankan-Scottish poet from Newcastle upon Tyne. She was part of the inaugural Poets of Colour Incubator Programme and was a Young Creative Associate with New Writing North. Ilisha was a Poet in Residence at the 2025 StAnza Poetry Festival and won the Futurist Award. She has been shortlisted for the James Berry Prize and Nine Arches Press' *Primers*. Her work has appeared in publications such as *Bi+ Lines Anthology*, *Butcher's Dog,* and *Third Space Anthology.*

WHAT SHE SAID

VERVE POETRY PRESS | £8.99 |

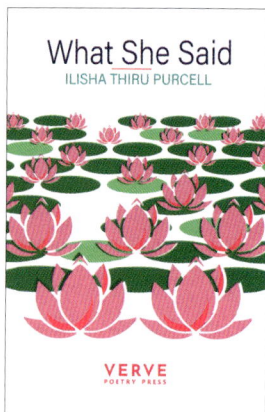

Writing against stasis, Edward Said's "travelling theory" re-establishes the travelling of ideas as a necessary medium for the emergence of new and different forms of knowledge, interpretations and reinterpretations. Ilisha Thiru Purcell's glorious pamphlet enacts the travelling that happens both before and after writing. Transposing classical Tamil love poetry, Akam poetry, into contemporary contexts, such as climate change, trauma, selfhood and sex, Purcell lucidly creates her own "landscapes" out of the remnants of this ever-changing world:

> Before becoming after
> is the hush of the hand
> felling a tree, the din of fingers
> that later pluck
> the splutters of growth.

In this multitude of voices, the personal and collective intersect in a chorus-like feat. At times it is the individual who laments that "all around there are limbs of tree." In other instances, animate and inanimate objects are given voice, as a way of questioning the futility of language and acknowledging the imminent dissolution of the world. While the book grapples with acutely urgent and cataclysmic themes, it does so with consummate attention to healing, "as if I speak the language of leaves". The ancestral thread that the poet refers to, and returns to, is the travelling back to "origins", to who we are as people and to the shared pain (and responsibility) that spans the planet we live in. By "unravelling" "secrets" and "shame", these poems reconstruct both the body and the world:

> On the shore I unravel
> the secrets that live under my skin.
>
> Shame is pleated around me like a sari
> that belonged to my mother,
> her mother and the mother of her.
>
> I place the frayed silk into the sea
> pray I do not turn back as I walk away.

This is a book to read and read again, for what it offers of poetry but also for us as we renew our vows to the planet. These are tender, reverberating, compassionate and non-complacent poems that powerfully usher in an exciting new poetic voice.

46   YOUSIF M. QASMIYEH & ALYCIA PIRMOHAMED

14. WHAT SHE SAID TO THE TREES

There were no passersby.
Only you saw the thief and what he took.

You who have been sapped of your speech
and wither as if ageing backwards.

I have my voice
but they look at me
as if I speak the language of leaves.

They turn from me and my browning tongue
as they turn from the truth of your withering.

AUTUMN BOOK REVIEWS

BEBE ASHLEY: HARBOUR DOUBTS
REVIEWED BY BETH DAVIES

Harbour Doubts is concerned with language barriers: between spoken and signed languages; between British and Irish Sign Language; between what the speaker says, what they want to say, and what they would rather leave unexpressed. In Ashley's poems, the frustrations of language learning and flawed communication provide a lens to explore isolation, longing, and the desire to shape one's own future, tempting us to almost believe the fragile hope that "in a different language, I can live a different life".

BANSHEE PRESS | £10.99 | PBS PRICE £8.20

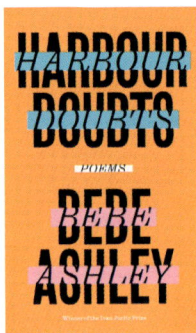

BILLY-RAY BELCOURT: THE IDEA OF AN ENTIRE LIFE
REVIEWED BY DAVE COATES

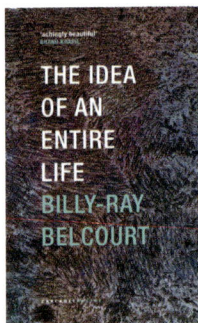

Belcourt's third collection has the breezy, casually devastating air of a 2am phone call with a very old friend. These poems communicate love, grief, dreams of home, intimacy and death with wit and grace, and are peppered with breathtaking turns of phrase and near-acrobatic thought, shifting from the abstract or spiritual to the cold-bucket concrete in an instant. Belcourt jokes, "we need (...) more / minor poets"; his book's local, familial frame and often blithe humour are underpinned by sincerely major questions.

CARCANET PRESS | £12.99 | PBS PRICE £9.75

SUZANNAH V. EVANS: UNDER THE BLUE
REVIEWED BY JASMINE GRAY

Riding the wave of its opening Baudelaire quotation, *Under the Blue* is a collage of the quiet horrors and ecstasies that form a life. Evans is tender, subtle and fierce in her exploration of all that cannot be expressed through language but must be attempted in any case. A poignant collection of prose poems painted on postcards – again and again, we are weighed down and made weightless by the brutal, beautiful reality of caring for those we love.

BLOOMSBURY | £12.99 | PBS PRICE £9.75

WRITING SQUAD & LEDBURY CRITICS

REVIEWED BY DAVE COATES

Kennard meditates on the hollowness of literary professionalism. Jonah, the reluctant prophet, is re-imagined as a mid-career hack, an insecure attendee of well-heeled junkets and conferences. The conceit's momentum dwindles, however, in a book that often lacks focus, and riffs for too long in similar emotional keys. Kennard is a witty, curious storyteller and a deft satirist, but this book limits itself, at times, with defensive self-deprecation and a reluctance to trust the reader with its ambitious imaginative leaps.

PICADOR | £12.99 | PBS PRICE £9.75

ARVIND KRISHNA MEHROTRA: OF LEAST CONCERN
REVIEWED BY SHASH TREVETT

Mehrotra's latest collection, written during lockdown, contains more of his masterful short lyric poems. Restricted to his garden, his thoughts are invaded by its fluidity. These are gentle poems, ruminating on the vast by concentrating on tiny particulars, like the hop of a tailorbird, the scuttle of a scorpion or the falling of a single brown leaf. A love song to nature, history and life, Mehrotra writes "To find / one's cadence / where one / is".

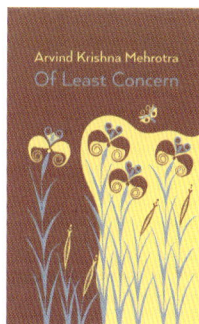

SHEARSMAN BOOKS | £12.95 | PBS PRICE £9.72

CHRIS McCABE: HEDONISM
REVIEWED BY GREGORY KEARNS

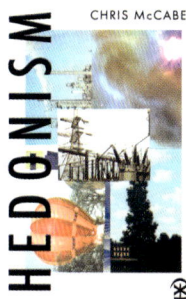

McCabe's *Hedonism* explores how we are othered from loved ones through death, how we are othered from the future through our political reality and how we are othered from understanding each other through the inexactness of language. He shows us the translative power of grief, "from the smile of a stranger / I remake my father." The collection is not just haunted by ghosts, but haunted by dreadnoughts, money and a poet reading his work to lions.

NINE ARCHES PRESS | £11.99 | PBS PRICE £9.00

BOOK REVIEWS

49

AGATA MASLOWSKA: WOMAN: PLANT: LANGUAGE
REVIEWED BY ROSE SCHIERIG

In this startling exploration of the complexities of belonging Maslowska navigates planes of ownership and freedom, addressing the natural world in its overlap with mankind to consider what is kept, what is withheld and what is shared. Identity is measured up against accessibility, unveiling the ways in which autonomy is challenged across language, womanhood and human experience. "Unlike your body / the sea belongs to no one." The body becomes a vehicle for ancestral memory and present day experience as Maslowska writes at the borders of violence and transformation.

BAD BETTY PRESS | £10.99 | PBS PRICE £8.25

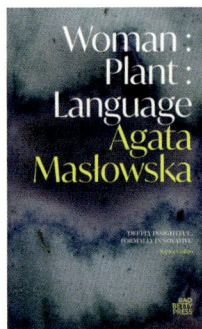

NINA MINGYA POWLES: IN THE HOLLOW OF THE WAVE
REVIEWED BY KAYLEIGH JAYSHREE

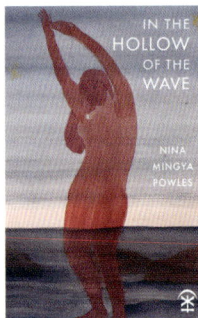

"The installation may feel surreal to the viewer, but this is not the artist's fantasy. It is her reality, her lived memory." With her ear close to seashells, fizzing pans and sterile museums, Nina Mingya Powles draws vivid textures and colours, looking at established forms, such as the sonnet. She engages in dialogue with Emily Berry and Virgina Woolf, using these conversations to blend her dreamscapes with discussions of othering, orientalism and closeness, while carefully choosing imagery, setting and epiphany.

NINE ARCHES PRESS | £11.99 | PBS PRICE £9.00

SUSAN NGUYEN: DEAR DIASPORA
REVIEWED BY DAVE COATES

Nguyen's great skill is investing small details – a shade of green, a radio station, a sparrow in the supermarket – with far-reaching significance, blending them into the book's ruminations on home, safety, beauty and hunger. A sequence on Vietnamese refugees renders the bodily impact of historical violence, its generational reverberations, disturbingly tangible and lends texture and colour to Nguyen's intimate studies of both her parents and her adolescent self: their particularities, desires, survival. A curious, empathetic and beautiful debut.

THE 87 PRESS | £14.99 | PBS PRICE £11.25

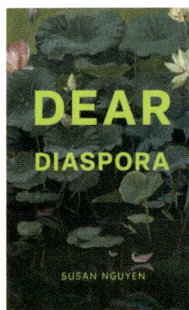

CLARE POLLARD: LIVES OF THE FEMALE POETS
REVIEWED BY NASIM REBECCA ASL

Pollard's latest collection spans the breadth of human creativity and creation. It's at once a joyous tribute to some of history's greatest female poets and to the smaller things that make a life – like cocktails, and head lice. These poems are physical and playful, bold yet delicate as we're swept along by references and allusions that dance off the page. It's poetry at its most confident. In the crescendoing titular poem Pollard's "saintly Poetess" deservedly finds her place in the canon she's honouring.

BLOODAXE BOOKS | £12.00 | PBS PRICE £9.00

DERYN REES-JONES: HÔTEL AMOUR
REVIEWED BY JENNY DANES

This book-length poem will leave its atmosphere in your body. Both its sections begin with a scene of liminality or dislocation: first, a woman stays in a Parisian hotel, and second, a woman maintains social distance from a joiner in her house ("Together they carried the distance as a child might an overfull glass of water.") From these nuclei, the book swings expansively through themes of illness, memory, bodies, grief and ageing. An inspiring example of how much poetry can hold.

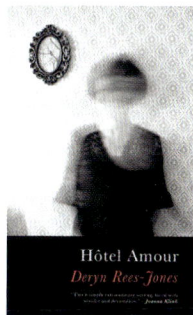

SEREN BOOKS | £12.99 | PBS PRICE £9.75

JESSICA TRAYNOR: NEW ARCANA
REVIEWED BY SHASH TREVETT

A hard-hitting collection, shaded with light and dark, which makes sense of the cruelty of life through the lens of cartomancy and the films of Tim Burton. Inventive and visceral, these poems are songs of grief, pointers of accusation, dissections of trauma and loss. The desperately tender poems in memory of a lost friend, Lydia, are countered by hopeful, gentle poems about the poet's daughters. A collection which looks at life askance, chronicling what occurs when "angel(s) / look away".

BLOODAXE BOOKS | £12.00 | PBS PRICE £9.00

PAMPHLET REVIEWS

Bower expresses her affection for bees in diverse poems ranging from bashful to blatant. Gender is a slippery construct that weaves itself throughout her work. At times, the idea hides in unsuspecting "he's" and "she's", or surfaces in pioneering female beekeepers, at others it presents itself bold and unforgiving: "Clip the wings / of your queen / with tiny scissors." A bittersweet meditation on bees, species extinction and our devastating impact on the natural world.

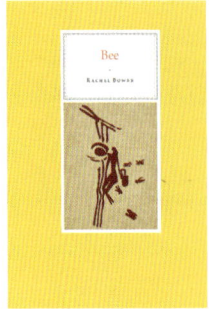

HAZEL PRESS   £12.00

RHIAN ELIZABETH: MAYBE I'LL CALL GILLIAN ANDERSON
REVIEWED BY MEGAN ROBSON

In this new pamphlet from Rhian Elizabeth, the speaker discovers compassion for her younger self by reflecting on her relationship with her daughter, who has newly flown the nest. Shot through with a sharp, modern sense of humour and the crisp, shimmering imagery of a Sofia Coppola film, this is a tender portrait of a woman who feels – as so many of us do – that she has yet to grow into herself.

BROKEN SLEEP BOOKS   £9.99

HASTI: YOUNG, DUMB AND FULL OF POEMS
REVIEWED BY MEGAN ROBSON

The speaker confesses they have been "navigating this world murkily", but future-gazing and science fiction form an empowering framework for reckoning with identity and the modern world in this trailblazing pamphlet, which is characterised by a deep humanity for all its cyborgs and spaceships. Hasti's confidence with form makes them unafraid to deviate from the rules, and the poem 'Neuroplastic' is a master-stroke. A wise and imaginative voice rises from this poet who is young, dumb and full of poems.

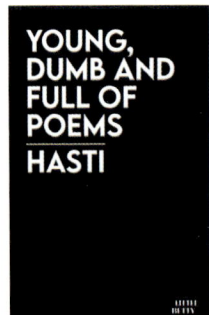

BAD BETTY PRESS   £7.50

| AUTUMN READING